PIANO
VOCAL
GUITAR

WORSHIP — THE ULTIMATE COLLECTION

WORSHIP

ISBN-13: 978-1-4234-1610-4
ISBN-10: 1-4234-1610-4

7777 W. BLUEMOUND RD. P.O. BOX 13819 MILWAUKEE, WI 53213

For all works contained herein:
Unauthorized copying, arranging, adapting, recording or public performance is an infringement of copyright.
Infringers are liable under the law.

Visit Hal Leonard Online at
www.halleonard.com

CONTENTS

4	Above All
14	Beautiful One
9	Better Is One Day
22	Blessed Be Your Name
29	Breathe
32	Come, Now Is The Time To Worship
38	Draw Me Close
46	Enough
52	God Of Wonders
41	Hallelujah (Your Love Is Amazing)
60	He Reigns
67	The Heart Of Worship
70	Here I Am to Worship
78	How Deep The Father's Love For Us
82	Hungry (Falling On My Knees)
73	I Could Sing Of Your Love Forever
93	Lord, I Lift Your Name On High
88	Lord, Reign In Me
96	Lord, You Have My Heart
100	Once Again
108	Open The Eyes Of My Heart
112	Shout To The North
120	Yesterday, Today And Forever
105	You Are My King (Amazing Love)

ABOVE ALL

Words and Music by PAUL BALOCHE and LENNY LeBLANC

© 1999 Integrity's Hosanna! Music/ASCAP (c/o Integrity Media, Inc., 1000 Cody Road, Mobile, AL 36695) and LenSongs Publishing/ASCAP
All Rights Reserved   International Copyright Secured   Used by Permission

8

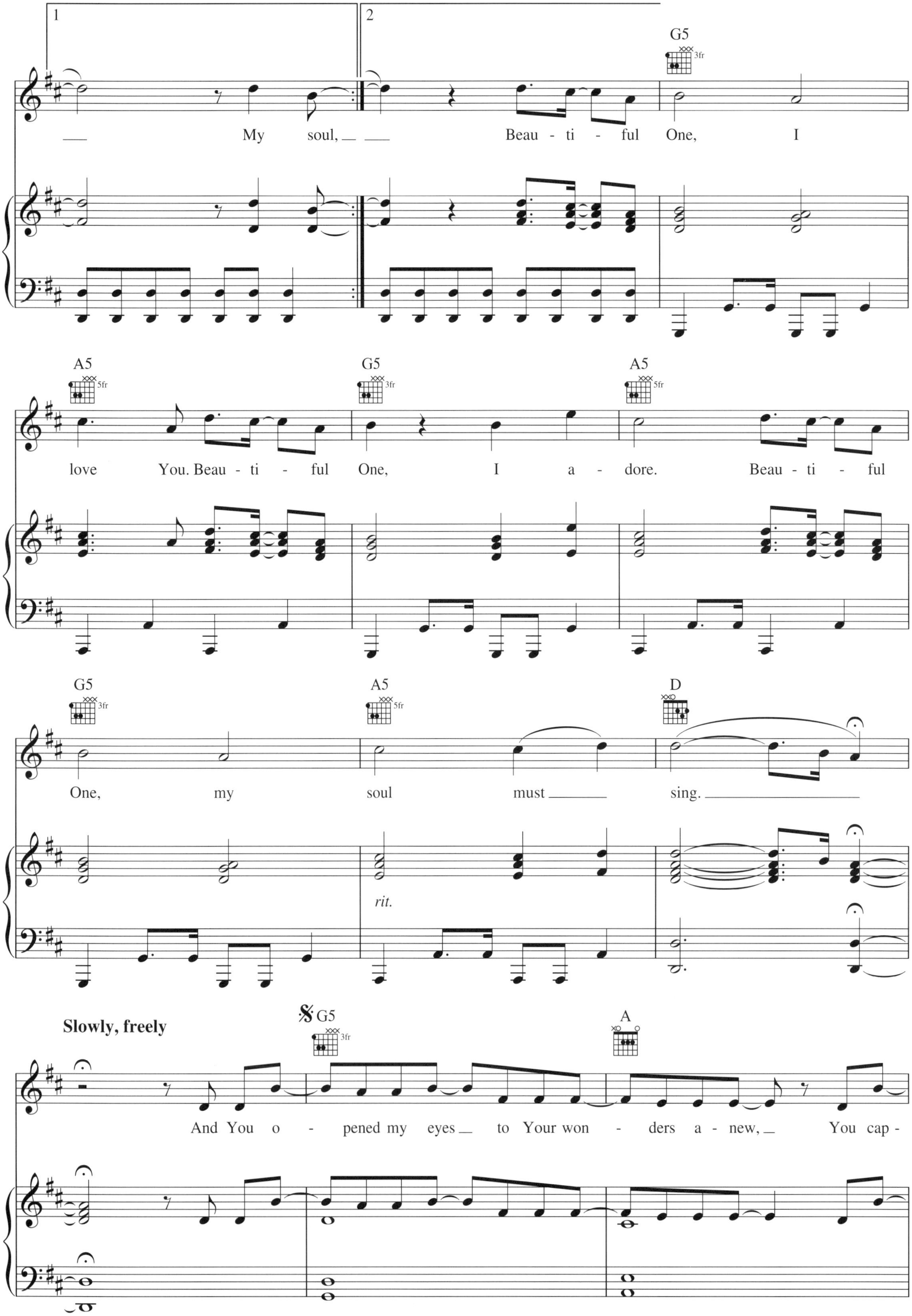
1
2
G5
A5
D
A
rit.
Slowly, freely
My soul, Beau - ti - ful One, I
love You. Beau - ti - ful One, I a - dore. Beau - ti - ful
One, my soul must sing.
And You o - pened my eyes to Your won - ders a - new, You cap -

BLESSED BE YOUR NAME

Words and Music by MATT REDMAN
and BETH REDMAN

*Recorded a half step lower.

© 2002 THANKYOU MUSIC (PRS)
Admin. Worldwide by EMI CMG PUBLISHING excluding Europe which is Admin. by kingswaysongs.com
All Rights Reserved   Used by Permission

BREATHE

Words and Music by
MARIE BARNETT

© 1995 MERCY/VINEYARD PUBLISHING (ASCAP)
Admin. in North America by MUSIC SERVICES o/b/o VINEYARD MUSIC GLOBAL INC.
All Rights Reserved   Used by Permission

COME, NOW IS THE TIME TO WORSHIP

Words and Music by
BRIAN DOERKSEN

* Recorded a half step lower.

© 1998 VINEYARD SONGS (UK/EIRE)
Admin. in North America by MUSIC SERVICES o/b/o VINEYARD MUSIC GLOBAL INC.
All Rights Reserved   Used by Permission

Em
C
your God,
G
G(add2)
G
come.
Oh, come.
(Come.)
G(add2)
G
G(add2)
Oh come, oh come.
(Come.)
Wor-ship the Lord, yeah.
G
G(add2)
G
(Come.)
Come, come, come.
(Come.)

DRAW ME CLOSE

Words and Music by
KELLY CARPENTER

Warmly
With pedal

Draw me close to You, never let me go. I lay it all down again to hear You say that I'm Your friend.

© 1994 MERCY/VINEYARD PUBLISHING (ASCAP)
Admin. in North America by MUSIC SERVICES o/b/o VINEYARD MUSIC GLOBAL INC.
All Rights Reserved Used by Permission

You are my desire, no one else will do. 'Cause nothing else could take Your place to feel the warmth of Your embrace. Help me find the way, bring me back to You.

B♭ F/B♭ E♭/B♭ B♭ F/A
You're all I want, You're all I've ev -
E♭/G F Gm7 F E♭ B♭/D
- er need - ed. You're all I want.
Cm7 F7 To Coda
1 B♭ F/B♭ E♭/B♭
2 B♭ E♭/F F D.S. al Coda
Help me know You are near.
CODA
B♭ F/G Gm7 Cm7 F7 B♭
Help me know You are near.
rit.

HALLELUJAH
(Your Love Is Amazing)

Words and Music by BRENTON BROWN
and BRIAN DOERKSEN

Joyfully

(1., 3.) Your love is a-maz-ing, stead-y and un-chang-ing. Your love is a moun-
(2.) -ing, I can feel it ris-ing, all the joy that's grow-

-tain, firm be-neath my feet. Your love is a mys-
-ing deep in-side of me. And ev-'ry time I see

-t'ry, how You gen-tly lift me when I am sur-round-
You, all Your good-ness shines through, and I can feel this God

© 2000 VINEYARD SONGS (UK/EIRE)
Admin. in North America by MUSIC SERVICES o/b/o VINEYARD MUSIC GLOBAL INC.
All Rights Reserved   Used by Permission

Dsus
Csus2
G
- ed, Your love car - ries me.
song ris - ing up in me.
Hal - le - lu - jah, Hal - le - lu -
D
Em7
Csus2
- jah, Hal - le - lu - jah,
Your love makes me sing, and Hal - le - lu -
G
D
Em7
- jah, Hal - le - lu - jah, Hal - le - lu - jah,
1, 2
Csus2
Your love makes me sing.
Your love is sur - pris -
Your love is a - maz -

43

G
D
Em7
- jah, Hal - le - lu - jah, Hal - le - lu - jah,
mp
Csus2
3fr
G
Your love makes_ me sing,_ and Hal - le - lu - jah, Hal - le - lu -
D
Em7
Csus2
3fr
- jah, Hal - le - lu - jah, Your love makes_ me sing,_ and Hal - le - lu -
cresc.
G
D
Em7
- jah, Hal - le - lu - jah, Hal - le - lu - jah,
mf

Csusz2
G
Your love makes _ me sing, _ and Hal - le - lu - jah, Hal - le - lu -
D
Em7
1
Csus2
- jah, Hal - le - lu - jah, Your love makes _ me sing, _ and Hal - le - lu-
2
Csus2
Your love makes _ me sing. _ Lord, You make _ me _
G
_ sing. How You make _ me _ sing.

ENOUGH

Words and Music by CHRIS TOMLIN
and LOUIE GIGLIO

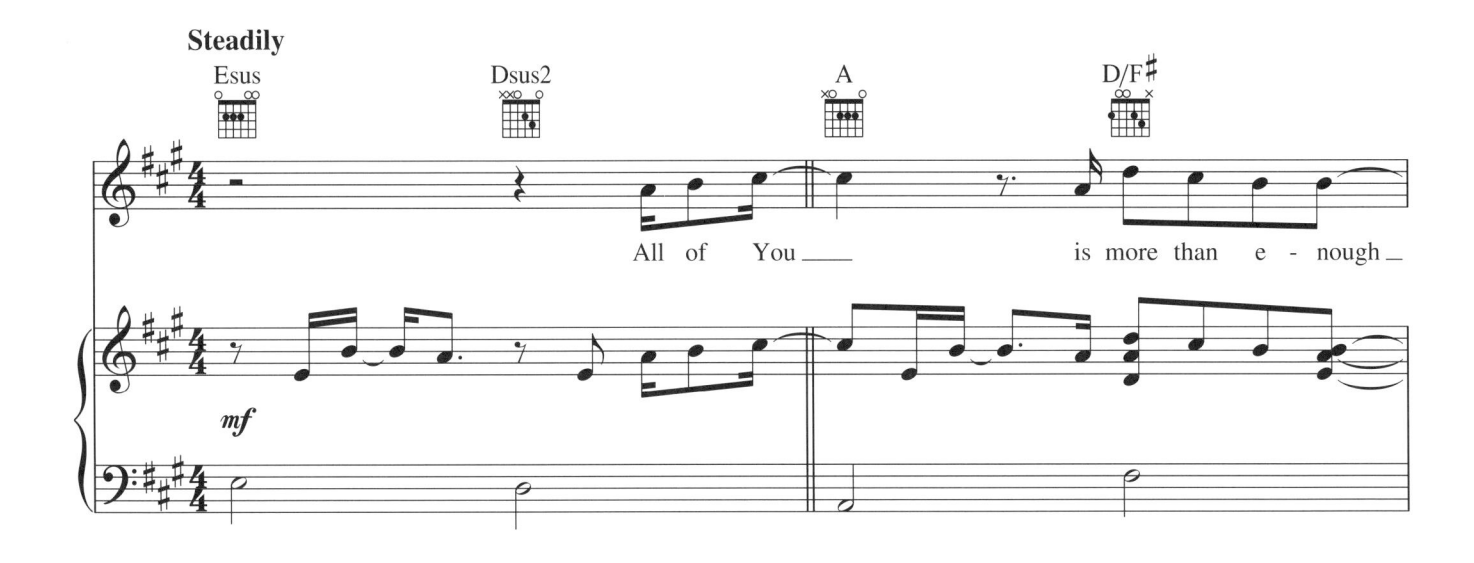

Steadily

All of You is more than e-nough for all of me, for ev-'ry thirst and ev-'ry need. You sat-is-fy me with Your love, and all I have in You

© 2002 WORSHIPTOGETHER.COM SONGS (ASCAP) and sixsteps Music (ASCAP)
Admin. by EMI CMG PUBLISHING
All Rights Reserved   Used by Permission

Esus A D/F♯ E Esus Dsus2
is more than e - nough.
A D/F♯ E Esus Dsus2 A Dsus2
You are my supply,
You're my sac - ri - fice
Esus A/C♯ D Bm7 E
my breath of life, and still more awe - some than I know.
of great - est price, and still more awe - some than I know.
A Dsus2 Esus A/C♯
You are my re - ward, worth liv - ing for,
You're the com - ing King, You are ev - 'ry - thing,

48

is more than e - nough. More than all I want, more than all I need. You are more than e - nough for me.

More than all __ I know, more than all __ I can say, __ You are more __ than e-nough. __ than e-nough. And all of You __ and all I have __ in You, __ and all I have __ in You __

Lyrics: is more than e-nough. All of You is more than e-nough for all of me.

Chords: Esus, Asus2, D/F#, Esus, D5, Asus2, D/F#, Esus, D5, Asus2, D/F#, Esus, D5, Asus2, D/F#, Esus, D5, Asus2

GOD OF WONDERS

Words and Music by MARC BYRD
and STEVE HINDALONG

Moderately

Lord of all cre-a-tion, of wa-ter, earth and sky, the heav-ens are Your tab-er-na-

© 2000 STORM BOY MUSIC (BMI), MEAUX MERCY (BMI), NEW SPRING (ASCAP) and NEVER SAY NEVER SONGS (ASCAP)
STORM BOY MUSIC and MEAUX MERCY Admin. by EMI CMG PUBLISHING
NEVER SAY NEVER SONGS Admin. by NEW SPRING
All Rights Reserved   Used by Permission

-cle; _____ glory to the Lord __ on __ high.

God of wonders beyond our __ galaxy, You are holy, __ holy. __ The universe __ declares __ Your __ Majesty; You are

54

holy, holy. Lord of heaven and earth,

Lord of heaven and earth.

Early in the morn-

-ing, I will celebrate the light.

Asus2
E5
2fr
Bsus
C♯m
When I stum - ble in the dark -
Asus2
E5
2fr
Bsus
C♯m
- ness,
I will lift Your Name by
Asus2
E5
2fr
night.
God of won - ders be - yond our gal - ax -
B5
F♯m11
C♯m7
Bsus
y,
You are ho - ly,
ho - ly.
The

un-i-verse_ de-clares_ Your_ Maj-es-ty; You are ho-ly,_ ho-ly._ Lord of heav-en and_ earth,_ Lord of heav-en and_ earth._ (Hal-le-lu-jah...)_ ...to the Lord of heav-en and_ earth._

...to the Lord of heav-en and earth.
(Hal - le - lu - jah...)

...to the Lord of heav-en and earth.
Hal - le - lu - jah...)

God of won-ders be-yond our gal-ax-y. You are

E
ho - ly,
ho - ly.
The un - i - verse declares Your Maj - es -
B/D♯
Asus2
C♯m7
Bsus
ty; You are ho - ly,
ho - ly.
E5
2fr
God of won - ders be - yond our gal - ax -
B5
F♯m11
y. You are ho - ly,

C♯m7
Bsus
E5
2fr
ho - ly. The un - i - verse de - clares Your Maj - es -
B5
Asus2
ty; You are ho - ly,
1
C♯m7
Bsus
ho - ly.
2
C♯m7
Bsus
ho - ly.
E5
2fr
1-3
4

HE REIGNS

Words and Music by PETER FURLER
and STEVE TAYLOR

Joyfully

song of the __ re- deemed __ rising from __ the Af- ri- can plain.
rise a- bove __ the four winds, caught up in __ the heav- en- ly sound.

© 2003 ARIOSE MUSIC (ASCAP) and SOYLENT TUNES (SESAC)
ARIOSE MUSIC Admin. by EMI CMG PUBLISHING
SOYLENT TUNES Admin. by ICG
All Rights Reserved   Used by Permission

G5
3fr
It's the
Let prais - es ech - o from the
F
C/E
song of the for - giv - en drown - ing out the Am - a - zon rain.
tow - ers of ca - the - drals to the faith - ful gath - ered un - der - ground.
G5
3fr
The song of
Of all the songs sung from the
F
C/E
A - sian be - liev - ers filled with God's ho - ly fire.
dawn of cre - a - tion, some were meant to per - sist.

It's ev-'ry tribe, ev-'ry tongue, ev-'ry na-tion; a love song born of a grate-ful choir.

Of all the bells rung from a thou-sand stee-ples, none rings tru-er than this.

It's all God's chil-dren sing-ing, "Glo-ry, glo-ry, hal-le-lu-jah! He reigns, He reigns!"

F
It's all God's chil - dren sing - ing, "Glo - ry, glo - ry,
C
G
1
hal - le - lu - jah! He reigns, He reigns."
Let it
2
F
It's all God's chil - dren sing - ing, "Glo - ry, glo - ry,
C
G
hal - le - lu - jah! He reigns, He reigns!"

64

powers__ of dark - ness can't drown__ out__ a sin - gle word.__ When all God's chil - dren sing out, "Glo - ry, glo - ry, hal - le - lu - jah! He reigns,__ He reigns!" All God's { (1.) chil - dren sing out, / (2.-4.) peo - ple sing - ing, } "Glo - ry, glo - ry,

C
G
1-3
hal - le - lu - jah! He reigns, __ He reigns!" All God's peo - ple sing - ing,
4
F
All God's chil - dren sing - ing, "Glo - ry, glo - ry,
C
G
hal - le - lu - jah! He reigns, __ He reigns!" All God's chil - dren sing - ing,
F
C/E
G
"Glo - ry, glo - ry, hal - le - lu - jah! He reigns!" __

THE HEART OF WORSHIP

Words and Music by
MATT REDMAN

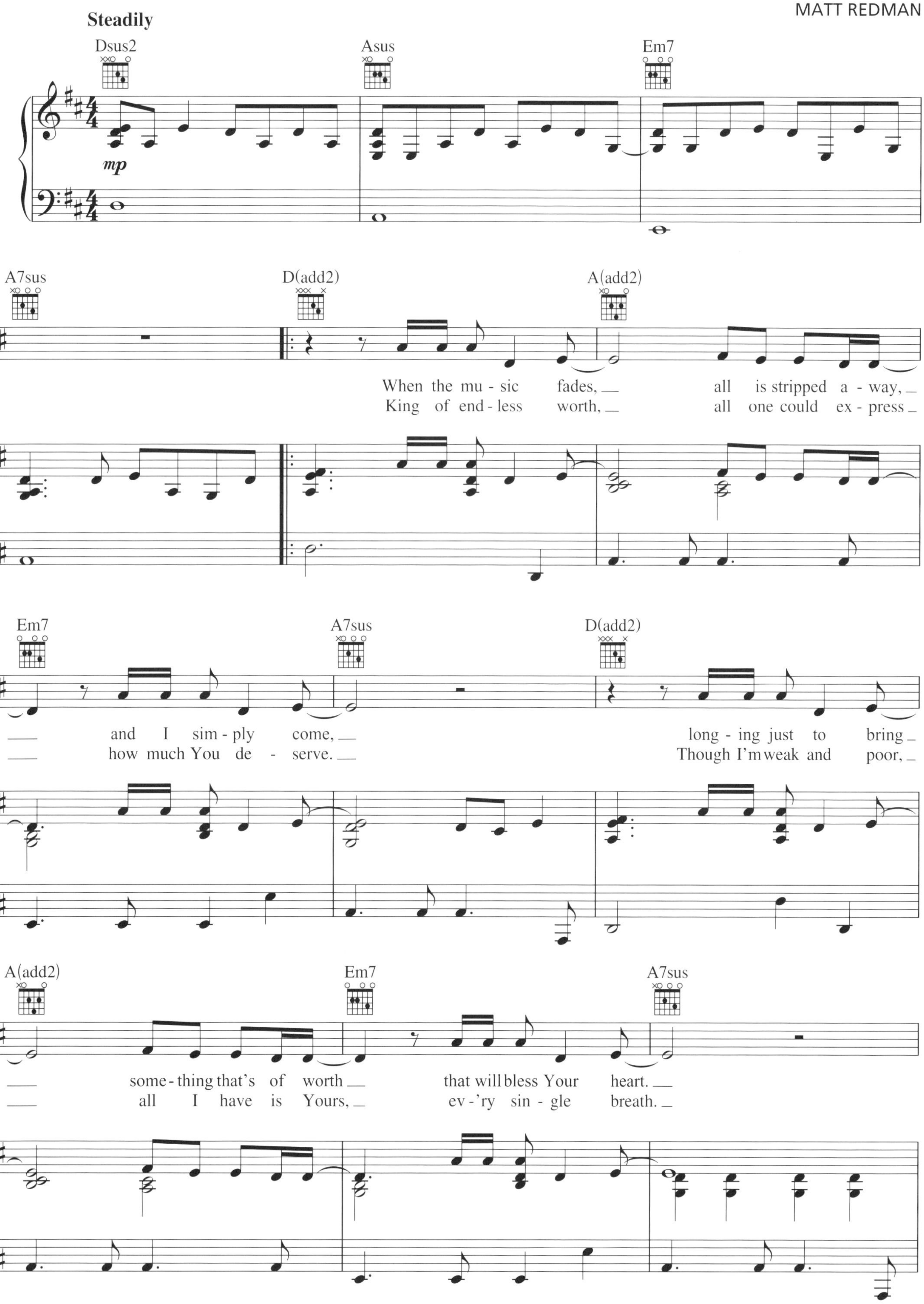

Em7
D/F♯
A7sus
I'll bring You more than a song, for a song in it - self
Em7
D/F♯
A7sus
Em7
D/F♯
is not what You have re - quired. You search much deep - er with - in
A7sus
Em7
D/F♯
through the way things ap - pear; You're look - ing in - to my heart.
A7sus
D(add2)
A/C♯
I'm com - ing back to the heart of wor - ship, and it's

Em9 D/F♯ Gmaj7 A7sus D(add2)
all a - bout You, all a - bout You, Je - sus. I'm sor - ry, Lord, for the thing
A/C♯ Em9 D/F♯
I've made it, when it's all a - bout You,
Gmaj7 A7sus
1
Dsus2 D/A A
all a - bout You, Je - sus.
Em7 A7sus
2
D

HERE I AM TO WORSHIP

Words and Music by
TIM HUGHES

Moderately slow

Light of the World, You stepped down into darkness,
King of all days, oh so highly exalted,
opened my eyes, let me see.
glorious in heaven above.
Beauty that made this
Humbly You came to the
heart adore You, hope of a life spent with You.
earth You created, all for love's sake became poor.

© 2001 THANKYOU MUSIC (PRS)
Admin. Worldwide by EMI CMG PUBLISHING excluding Europe which is Admin. by Kingswaysongs.com
All Rights Reserved Used by Permission

Here I am to wor-ship, here I am to bow down, here I am to say that You're my God. You're al-to-geth-er love-ly, al-to-geth-er wor-thy, al-to-geth-er won-der-ful to me.

And I'll nev-

B/D♯
E/G♯
A
Asus2
B/D♯
E/G♯
4fr
- er know how much it cost to see my sin up - on
1
2
A
Asus2
A
Asus2
D.S. al Coda
that cross. And I'll nev - that cross. Here I am to
CODA
Asus2
B7sus
2fr
E

I COULD SING OF YOUR LOVE FOREVER

Words and Music by
MARTIN SMITH

F
Gm11
3 fr
B♭sus2
6 fr
I could sing, ___
Csus
3 fr
F
Gm11
3 fr
I could sing of Your love for - ev -
B♭sus2
6 fr
Csus
3 fr
er.
2
Csus
3 fr
when Your love came down, yeah. _
F(add2)
Gm11
3 fr
B♭(add2)
I could sing of Your love ___ for - ev - er,
I could sing of Your love _

C
F(add2)
Gm11
3 fr
for - ev - er, I could sing of Your love for - ev - er,
B♭(add2)
C
F(add2)
I could sing of Your love for - ev - er. (I could sing of Your love
Gm11
3 fr
B♭(add2)
C
for - ev - er, I could sing of Your love for - ev - er,
F(add2)
Gm11
3 fr
B♭(add2)
I could sing of Your love for - ev - er, I could sing of Your love

forever.) Oh, I feel like dancing; it's foolishness, I know. But when the world has seen the light they will dance with joy like we're dancing now, yeah. -ing now, yeah.

77

HOW DEEP THE FATHER'S LOVE FOR US

Words and Music by
STUART TOWNEND

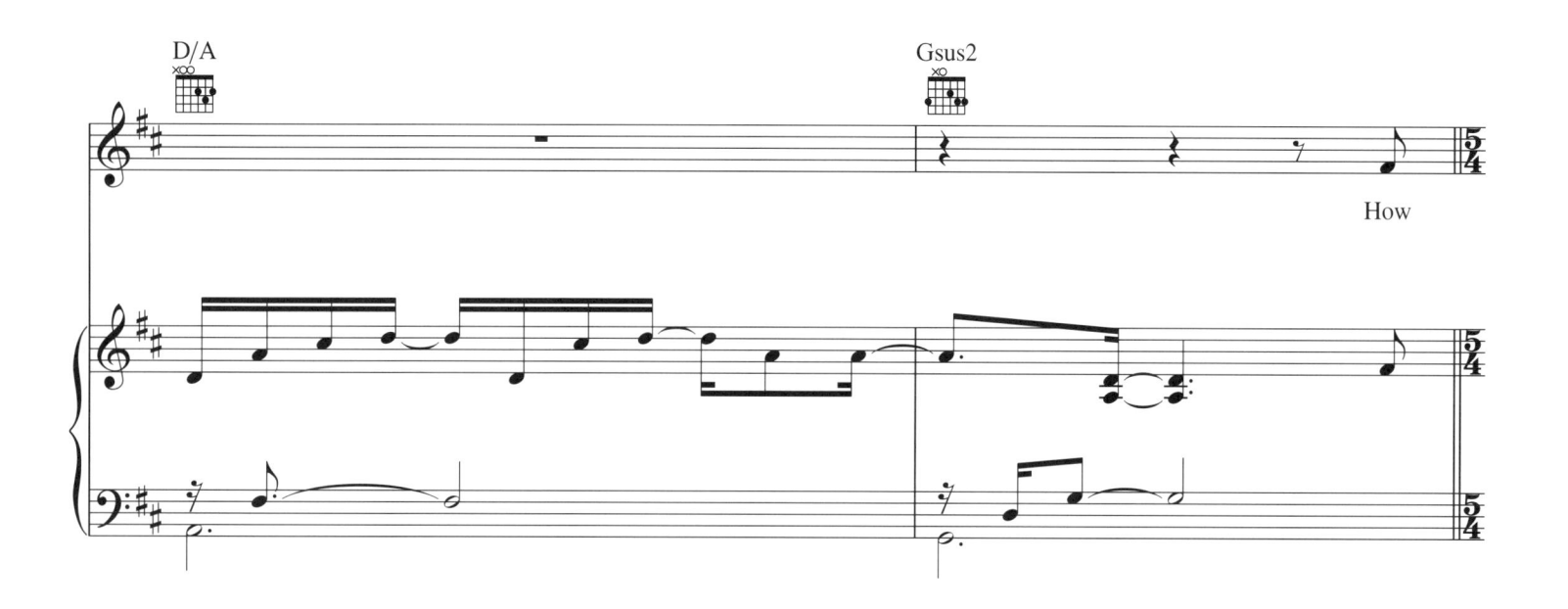

Slowly

*How
deep the Fa-ther's love for us; how vast be-yond all meas-ure that
hold the man up-on a cross, my sin up-on His shoul-ders. A-
will not boast in an-y-thing, no gifts, no pow'r, no wis-dom, but*

© 1995 THANKYOU MUSIC (PRS)
Admin. Worldwide by EMI CMG PUBLISHING excluding Europe which is Admin. by kingswaysongs.com
All Rights Reserved   Used by Permission

D Em7 D/F♯ G(add9) D/F♯ A D
He should give His on - ly Son to make a wretch His treas - ure. How
shamed, I hear my mock - ing voice call out a - mong the scoff - ers. It
I will boast in Je - sus Christ, His death and res - ur - rec - tion. What
D Em7 D/F♯ G(add9) D/F♯ Bm7 A
great the pain of sear - ing loss. The Fa - ther turns His face a - way as
was my sin that held Him there un - til it was ac - com - plished. His
should I gain from His re - ward? I can - not give an an - swer, but
D Em7 D/F♯ G(add9) D/F♯ A
wounds which mar the Cho - sen One bring man - y sons to glo -
dy - ing breath has brought me life. I know that it is fin -
this I know with all my heart: His wounds have paid my ran -

ry.
ished.

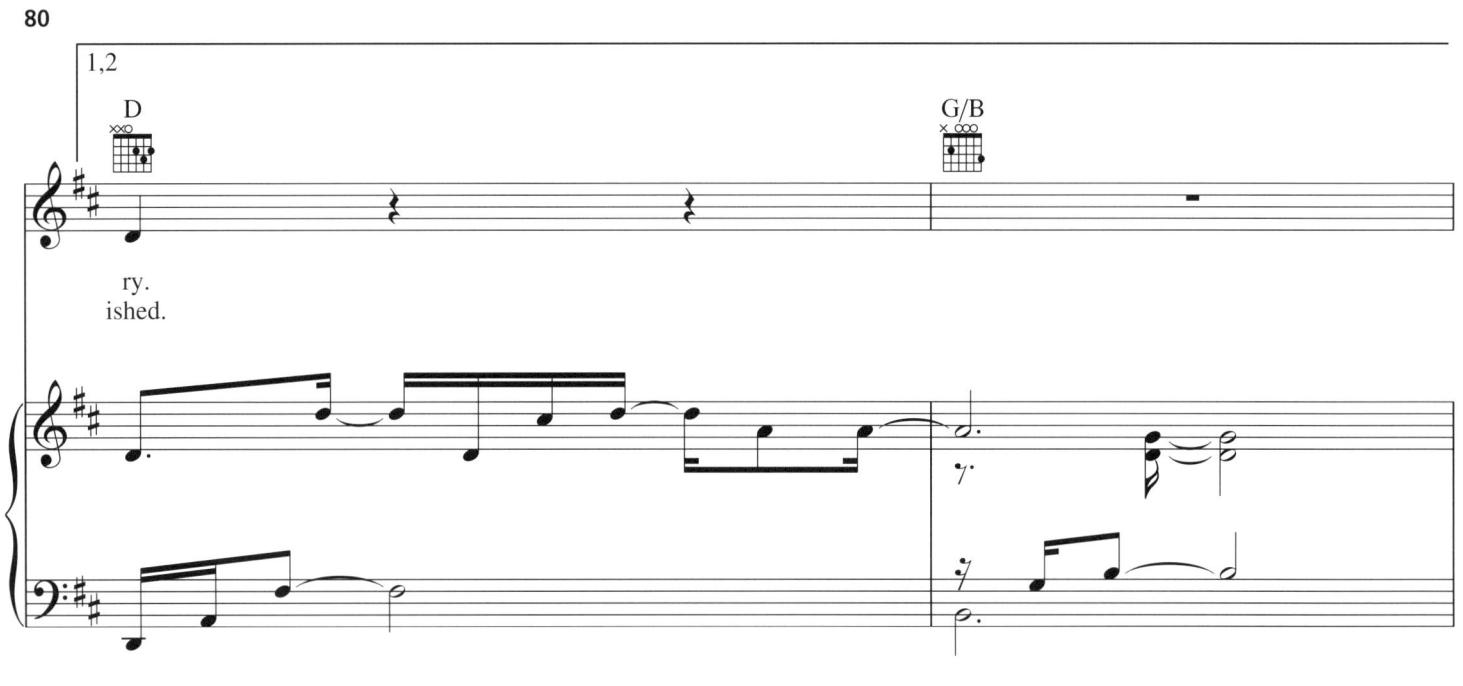

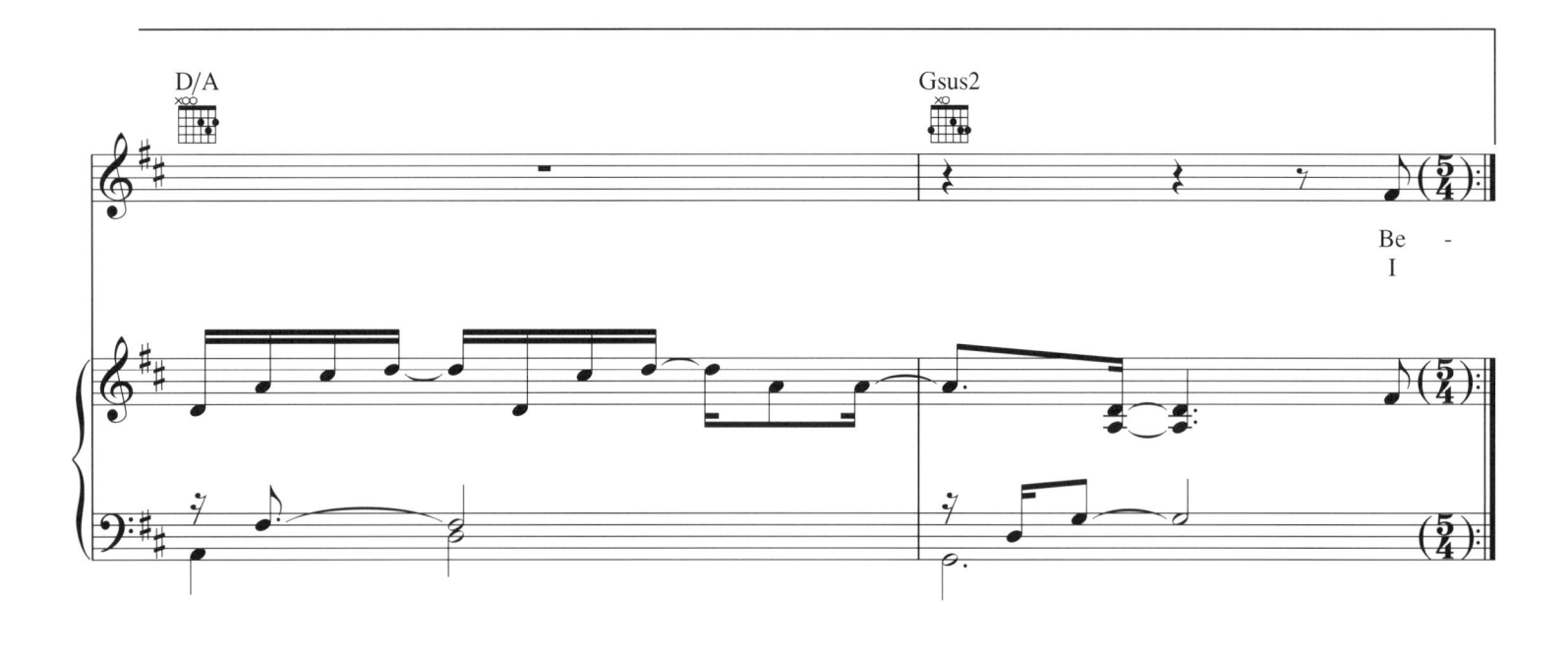

Be -
I

som. What should I gain from His re - ward? I

81

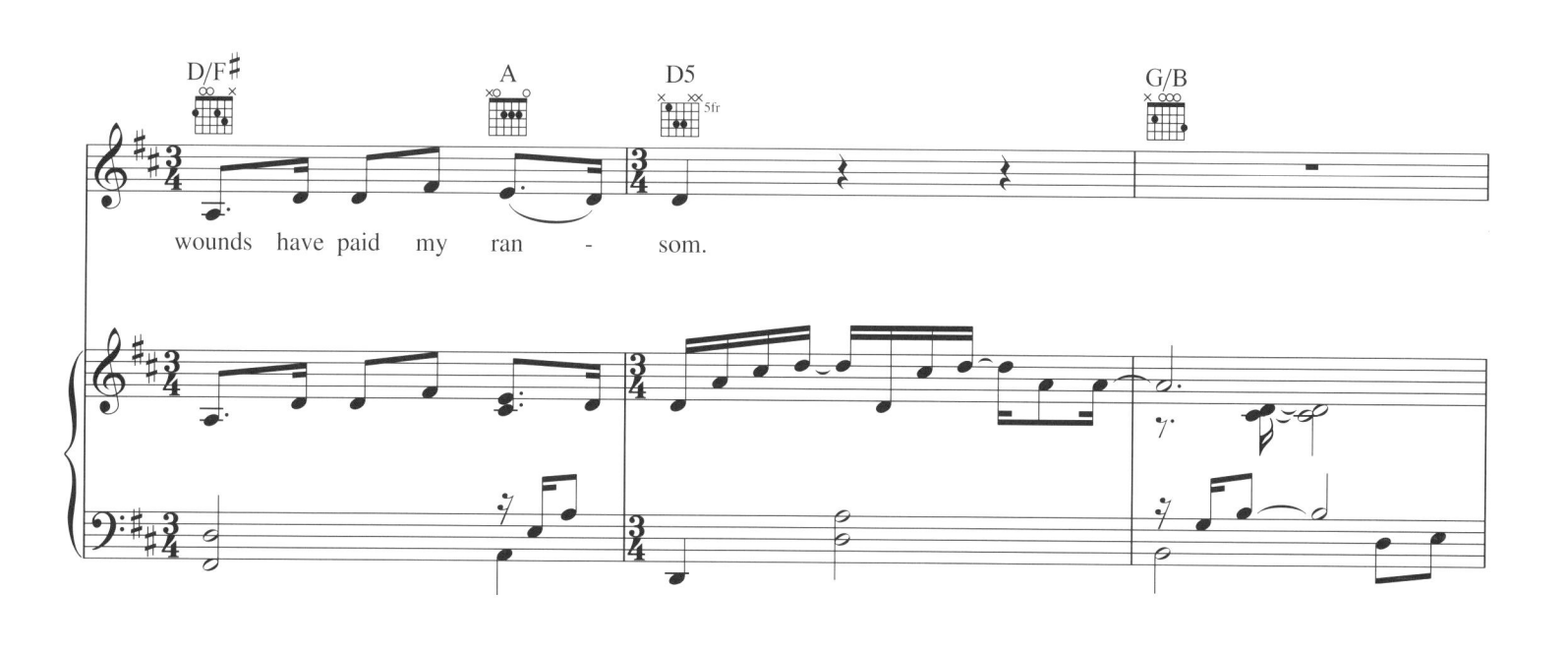

can - not give an an - swer, but this I know with all my heart: His wounds have paid my ran - som.

HUNGRY
(Falling on My Knees)

Words and Music by
KATHRYN SCOTT

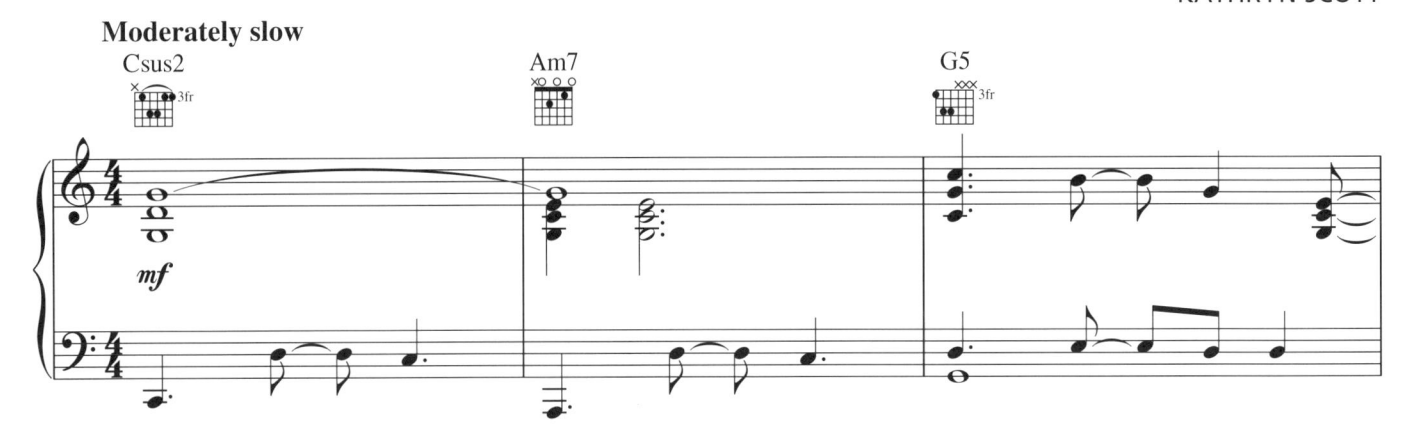

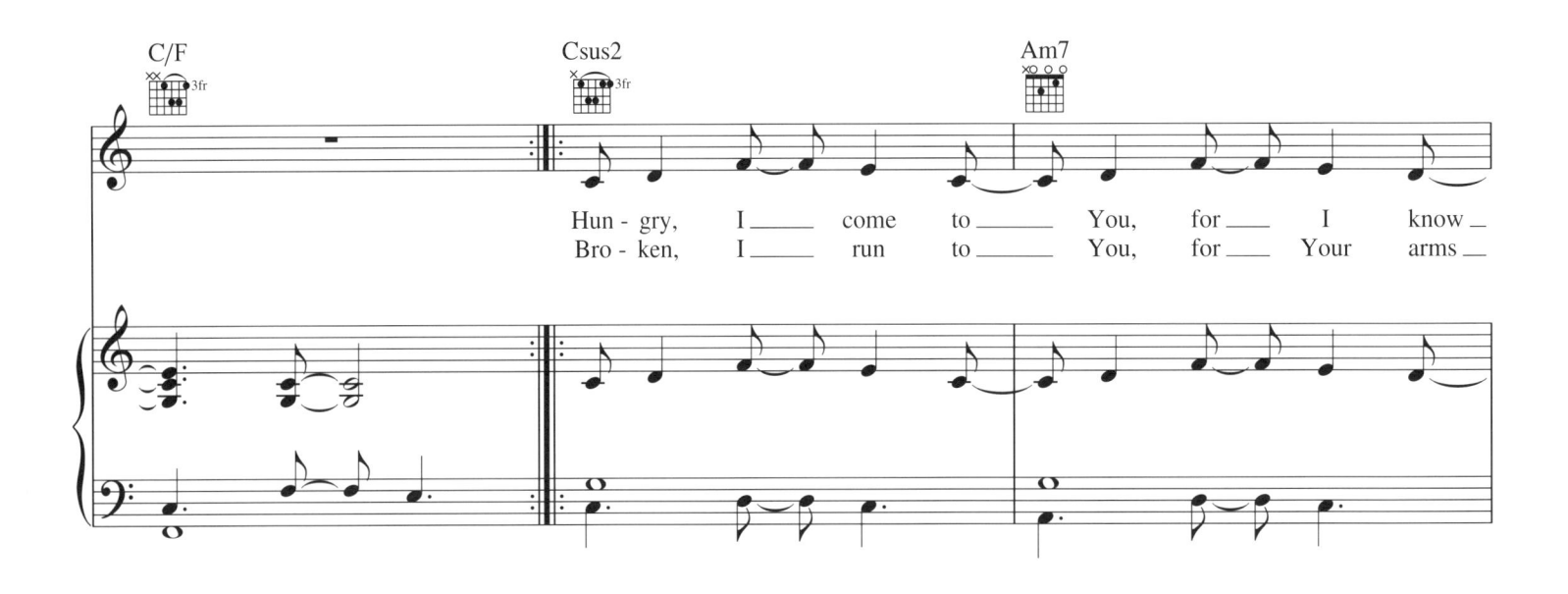

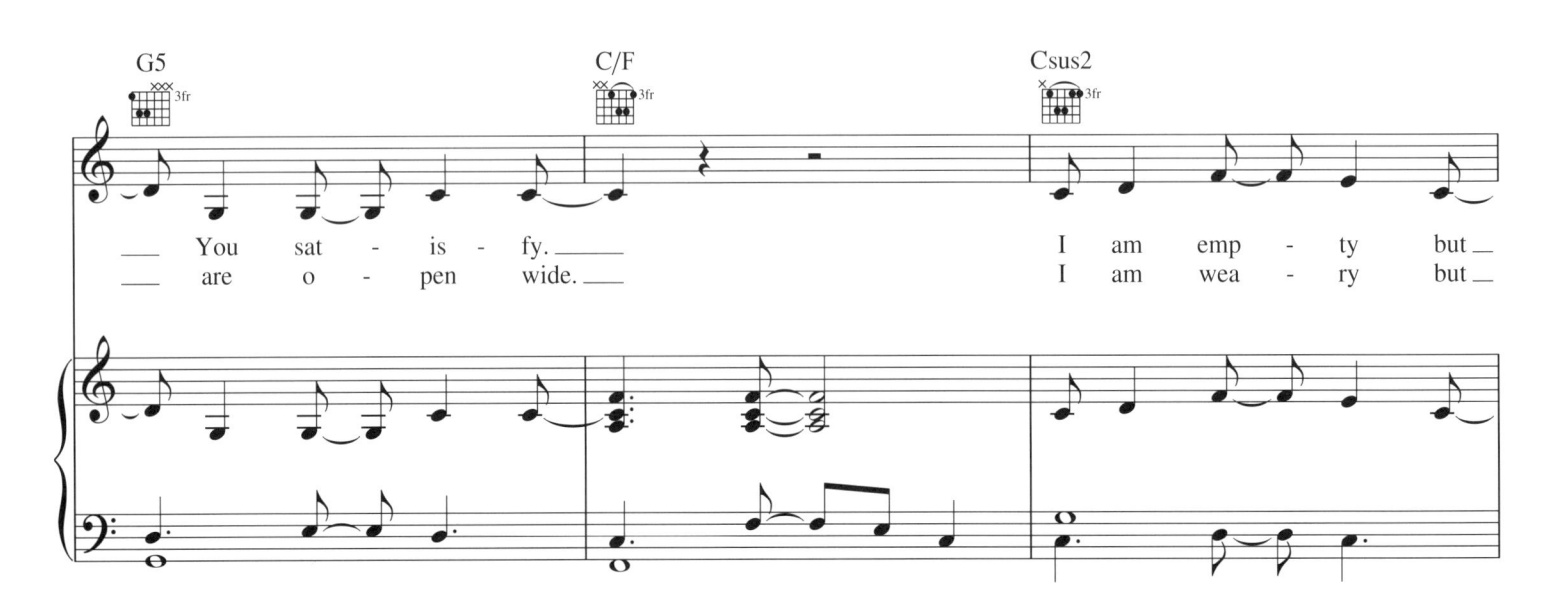

Moderately slow

Hun - gry, I come to You, for I know You sat - is - fy. I am emp - ty but
Bro - ken, I run to You, for Your arms are o - pen wide. I am wea - ry but

© 1999 VINEYARD SONGS (UK/EIRE)
Admin. in North America by MUSIC SERVICES o/b/o VINEYARD MUSIC GLOBAL INC.
All Rights Reserved   Used by Permission

I know Your love does not run dry.
I know Your touch restores my life. So I

wait for You. So I wait for You.

I'm falling on my knees, offer-

-ing all of me. Jesus, You're all this heart

Fmaj7
1
Csus2
3fr
Am7
is liv - ing for.
G5
3fr
C/F
3fr
2,3
C5
3fr
Fmaj9
C
Cmaj7
Fmaj7
F6/9
I'm fall - ing on my knees, of - fer -
C
Cmaj7
Fmaj7
F6/9
C
Cmaj7
- ing all of me. Je - sus, You're all this heart

is liv-ing for.

So I wait for You.

F/A
G5
3fr
Fsus2
So I wait for You.
So I
G
F/A
G/B
wait for You.
So I wait for You,
Fsus2
D.S. al Coda
(take 3rd ending)
and I'm fall -
CODA
Csus2
3fr
(2.) Vocals tacet
Am7
G5
3fr
C/F
3fr

87

LORD, REIGN IN ME

Words and Music by
BRENTON BROWN

Over all the earth, You reign on high.
Over ev'ry thought, over ev'ry word,
Ev'ry mountain stream, ev'ry sunset sky.
may my life reflect the beauty of my Lord.

(1.,3.) But my one request, Lord, my only aim
(2.) 'Cause You mean more to me than any earthly thing,

© 1998 VINEYARD SONGS (UK/EIRE)
Admin. in North America by MUSIC SERVICES o/b/o VINEYARD MUSIC GLOBAL INC.
All Rights Reserved   Used by Permission

89

is that You'd reign in me a - gain.
so won't You reign in me a - gain?

Lord, reign in me. Reign in Your pow'r,

o - ver all my dreams, in my dark - est hour,

'cause You are the Lord of all I am,

so won't You reign in me a - gain?

O - ver all the earth You reign on high. Ev - 'ry moun - tain stream, ev - 'ry sun - set sky.

D.S. al Coda

91

Lord, reign in me. Reign in Your pow'r, over all my dreams, in my darkest hour. You are the Lord of all I am, so won't you reign in me a-gain? Won't you reign, won't you

F G Dm7 F G
reign in me a - gain? Come and reign, Lord; won't You reign in me a - gain?
C G Fmaj7 F/G C G
Hey, yeah, yeah, yeah, mm.
F6 F/G C G F6 F/G
Hey, yeah, yeah, yeah.
Slower
C G F6 F/G C
rall.

LORD, I LIFT YOUR NAME ON HIGH

Words and Music by
RICK FOUNDS

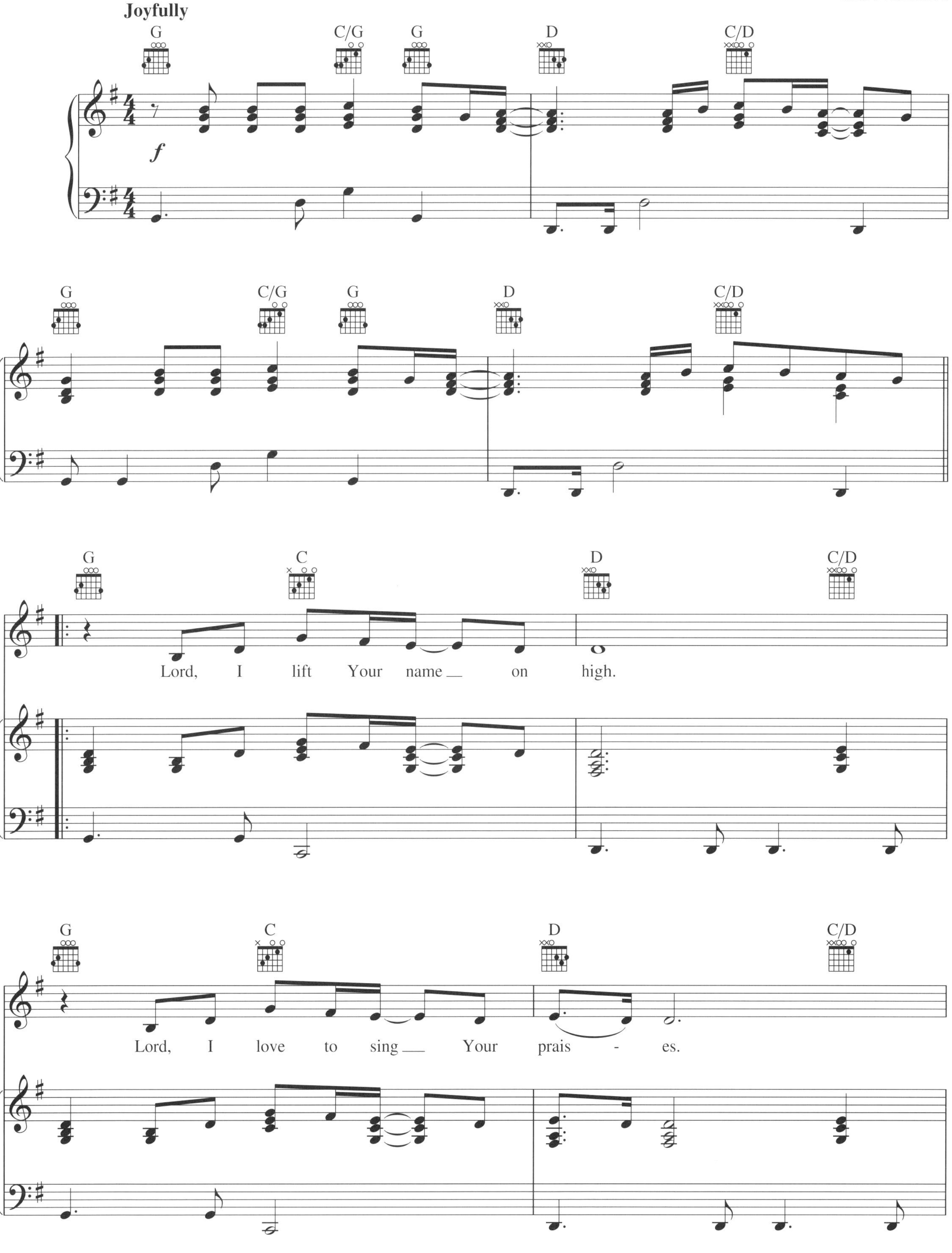

| G | C | D | C/D |

I'm so glad You're in my life,

| G | C | C/D D | C/D D |

I'm so glad You came to save us.

%
| G | C | D | C |

You came from heav-en to earth to show the way,

| G | C | D | C |

from the earth to the cross my debt to pay.

G C D Em7
From the cross to the grave, from the grave to the sky,
Am7 C/D D7
To Coda
1 G D/G C/G
2 G C/D D
D.S. al Coda
Lord, I lift Your name on high.
high.
CODA
G G/B C C/D D7
high. Lord, I lift Your name on
G Bm7 C C/D D7 G
high. Lord, I lift Your name on high.

LORD, YOU HAVE MY HEART

Words and Music by
MARTIN SMITH

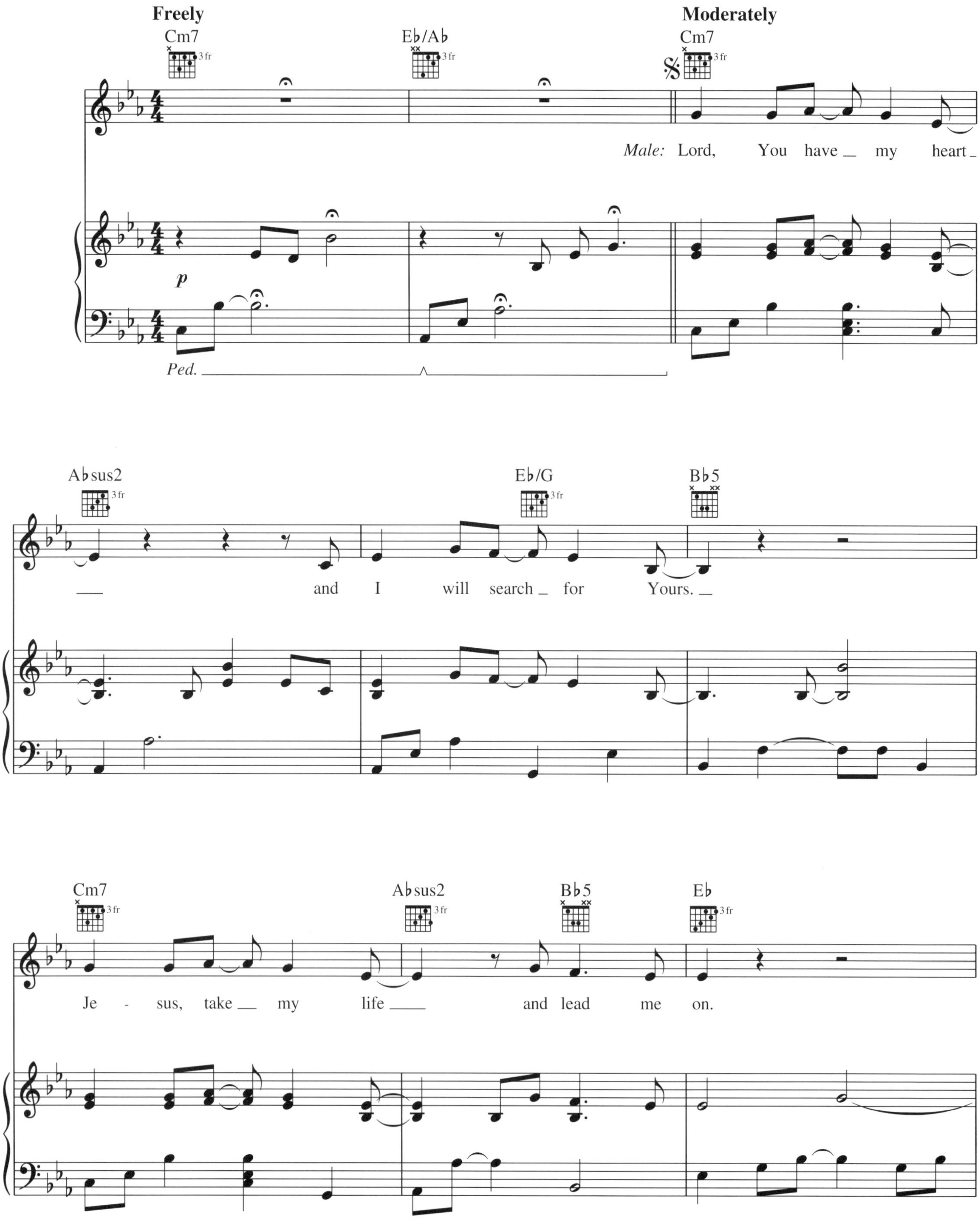

B♭/D
Cm7
A♭sus2
Lord, You have my heart and
E♭/G
B♭5
Cm7
I will search for Yours. Let me be to You
To Coda
A♭sus2
B♭5
E♭
E♭
a sac - ri - fice. And I will
A♭sus2
E♭/G
B♭5
B♭sus
B♭
E♭
praise You, Lord, and I will

Absus2
Eb/G
Bb5
3 fr
sing of love come down.
And
Eb
Absus2
Eb/G
Bb5
as You show Your face,
we'll
Absus2
Eb/G
Bb5
Eb
Bb/D
D.S. al Coda
see Your glo - ry here.
CODA
Eb
Absus2
Eb/G
I will praise You, Lord,
Female: (I will

99

ONCE AGAIN

Words and Music by
MATT REDMAN

Moderately

Jesus Christ, I think upon Your sacrifice; You became nothing, poured out to death.
Now You are exalted to the highest place, King of the heavens, where one day I'll bow.

© 1995 THANKYOU MUSIC (PRS)
Admin. Worldwide by EMI CMG PUBLISHING excluding Europe which is Admin. by kingswaysongs.com
All Rights Reserved   Used by Permission

E B/E A E/G♯ F♯m7 B
Man - y times I've won - dered at Your gift of life; I'm in that place once a - gain.
But for now, I mar - vel at this sav - ing grace; I'm full of praise once a - gain.
E F♯m7 B E
I'm in that place once a - gain.
I'm full of praise once a - gain.
And
E/G♯ A(add2) E/G♯ B E/G♯ A(add2)
once a - gain I look up - on the cross where You died. I'm hum - bled by Your mer - cy and I'm
E/G♯ B C♯m7 A 1 E/G♯ B
bro - ken in - side. Once a - gain I thank You, once a - gain I pour out my life.
4fr

E Esus E Esus2 E Esus
E Esus2
2
E/G♯ B A B
once a-gain I pour out my life. Oh, I pour out my life.
E Esus2 E/G♯ A(add2) E/G♯ B
And once a-gain I look up-on the cross where You died. I'm
E/G♯ A(add2) E/G♯ B C♯m7 4fr A
thank-ful for Your mer-cy and I'm bro-ken in-side. Once a-gain I thank You,

once a-gain I pour out my life.

Thank You for the cross, thank You for the cross, thank You for the cross, my

Friend. Thank You for the cross, thank You for the cross, thank You for the cross, my Friend. Friend.

My Friend.
(Vocal 1st time only)

YOU ARE MY KING
(Amazing Love)

Words and Music by
BILLY JAMES FOOTE

Worshipfully

I'm for-giv-en _____ be-cause You were _ for-sak-en.
I'm ac-cept-ed; You were _ con-demned. _ I'm a-live _ and well; _ Your
Spir-it is _ with-in _ me be-cause You died _ and rose _ a-gain. _

© 1999 WORSHIPTOGETHER.COM SONGS (ASCAP)
Admin. by EMI CMG PUBLISHING
All Rights Reserved   Used by Permission

A-maz-ing love, __ how __ can it be __ that You, my __ King, __ would die __ for me? __

A-maz-ing love, __ I __ know it's true; __

it's my __ joy __ to hon - or You. __

In all __ I __ do, __ I hon - or You. __

107

You are my King. You are my King. Jesus, You are my King. Jesus, You are my King.

D.S. al Coda
(with repeats)

CODA

Asus A G A D

In all I do, I honor You.

OPEN THE EYES OF MY HEART

Words and Music by
PAUL BALOCHE

Driving Rock

O-pen the eyes of my heart, Lord, won't You o-pen the eyes of my heart? 'Cause I want to

*Recorded a half step lower.

© 1997 Integrity's Hosanna! Music/ASCAP
c/o Integrity Media, Inc., 1000 Cody Road, Mobile, AL 36695
All Rights Reserved   International Copyright Secured   Used by Permission

C/G
G
see You, yes, I want to see You.
Gm7
C/G
G
O-pen the eyes of my heart, Lord, won't You
D/G
C/G
o-pen the eyes of my heart, 'cause I want to see You,
G
yes, I want to see You. To see You

high and lift-ed up, shin-ing in the light of Your glo-

-ry. Pour out Your pow'r and love, as we sing,

"Ho-ly, ho-ly, ho-ly."

111

SHOUT TO THE NORTH

Words and Music by
MARTIN SMITH

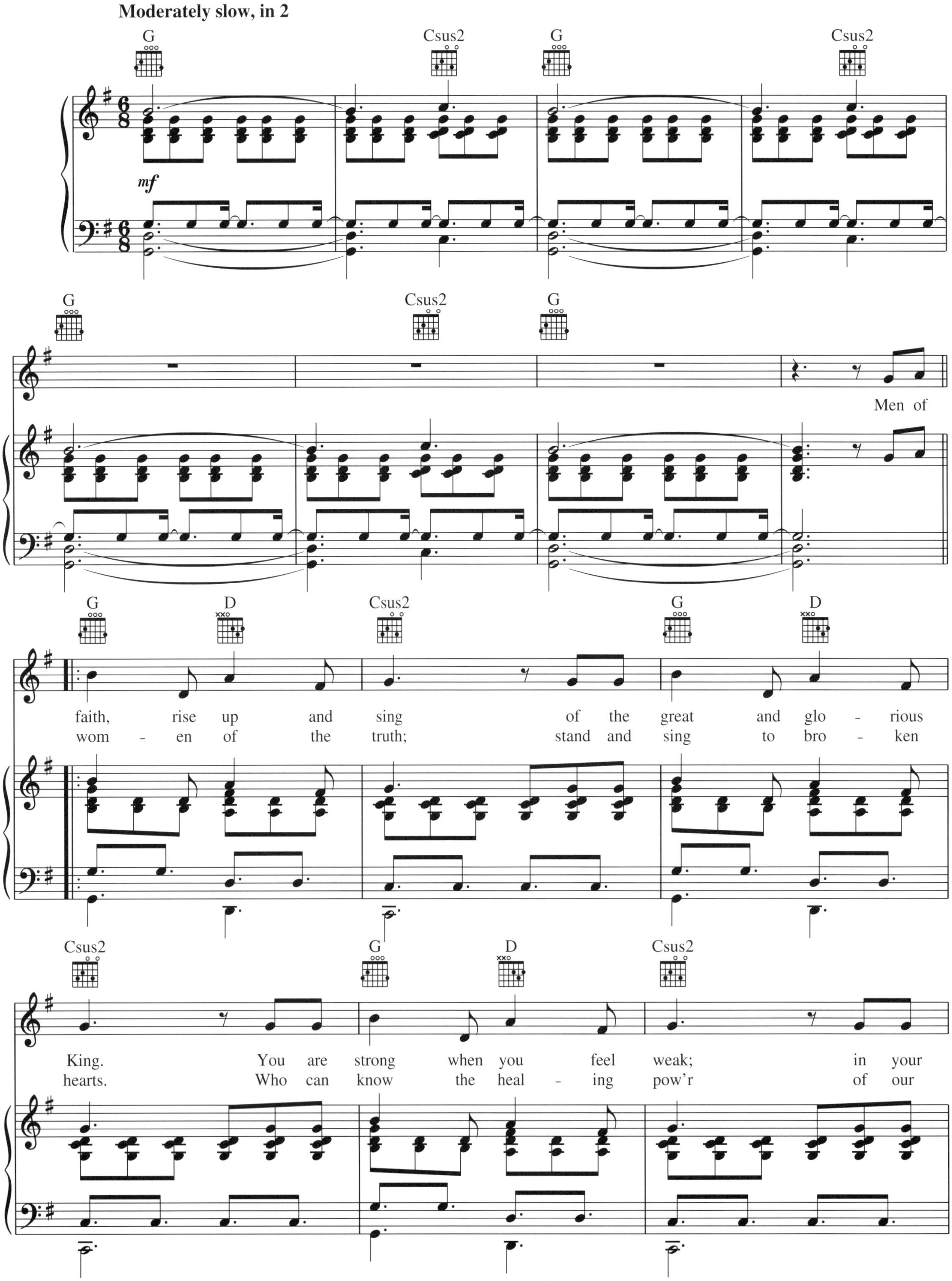

brokenness, complete.
awesome King of love?

Shout to the north and the south; sing to the east and the west. Jesus is Savior to all, Lord of heaven and earth.

Rise up,

earth. We will shout to the north and the south, sing to the east and the west. Je-sus is Sav-ior to all, Lord of heav-en and earth. We've been through fi-re, we've been through rain, we've been re-fined by the

pow'r of His name. We've fall-en deep-er in love with You; You've burned the truth on our lips. We will shout to the north and the south, sing to the east and the west. Je-sus is Sav-ior to all, Lord of heav-en and earth. We will shout to the north and the south, sing to the east and the west. Je-sus is Sav-ior to all, Lord of heav-en and earth. Rise up, church, with bro-ken wings; fill this place with songs a-gain, of our

| G | D | Csus2 | G | D |

God who reigns on high. By His grace, a-gain we'll

| Csus2 | | G |

fly. _____ *Children:* Shout to the

| C | D | G | C | D |

north and the south; sing to the east and the west.

| G | C | D | C | D |

Je-sus is Savior to all, Lord of heav-en and

earth. *All:* We will shout to the north and the south, sing to the east and the west. Je-sus is Sav-ior to all, Lord of heav-en and earth. Shout to the north and the south; sing to the *east and the west. Je-sus is Sav-ior to all*

Lord of heav-en and earth. We will earth. Oh,___

Lord of heav-en and earth. Oh,___ Lord of heav-en and

earth. Oh,___ Lord of heav-en and earth.

YESTERDAY, TODAY AND FOREVER

Words and Music by
VICKY BEECHING

Moderately fast

Ev-er-last-ing God, the years go by, but You're un-chang-ing. In this fra-gile world, You
Un-cre-at-ed One, You have no end and no be-gin-ning. Earth-ly pow-ers fade, but

© 2003 THANKYOU MUSIC (PRS)
Admin. Worldwide by EMI CMG PUBLISHING excluding Europe which is Admin. by kingswaysongs.com
All Rights Reserved   Used by Permission

B♭
Dm7
Gm11
are the only firm foundation.
there is no end to Your kingdom.
Always loving, always true,
F/A
B♭6/9
always merciful and good, so good.
Dm7
C(add4)
F/A
B♭
Dm
C
Yesterday, today and forever,

F/A Bb Dm C
You are the same; You never change.
F/A Bb Dm C Gm7
Yesterday, today and forever, You are faithful and
1
Bb5 Csus F/A Bb Dm C
we will trust in You. We will trust in You.
F/A Bb Dm C
2
Bb5 Csus
we will trust You.
3fr

123

Yes - ter - day, to - day and for - ev - er,
You are the same; You nev - er change.
Yes - ter - day, to - day and for - ev - er, You are faith - ful and
we will trust in You. We will trust in You.

F/A
B♭(add2)
3fr
We will trust in You,
F/A
in You.
B♭maj13
F/A
Yah - weh,
God un -
firm foun -
1
2
B♭maj13
chang - ing.
da - tion. You are Yah - weh,

F/A
1
God un - chang - ing. You are
firm foun -
2
F/A Bb Dm C
da - tion. Yes - ter - day, to - day and for - ev - er,
F/A Bb Dm C
You are the same; You nev - er change.
F/A Bb Dm C
Yes - ter - day, to - day and for - ev - er,

Gm7
B♭
B♭6
You are faithful and we will trust in You.
F/A
B♭sus2
Dm7
Csus
We will trust in You.
F/A
B♭sus2
Dm7
Csus
F/A
B♭sus2
We will trust in You.
Dm7
Csus
F/A
B♭sus2
You are a faithful God, faith-
3fr

Dm7
Csus
F/A
B♭sus2
- ful, faith - ful, faith - ful God.
We will trust in You.
We will trust in You,
faith - ful God,
C(add4)
faith - ful God.
3fr

More Contemporary Christian Folios from Hal Leonard

Arranged for Piano, Voice and Guitar

THE VERY BEST OF AVALON – TESTIFY TO LOVE
All 16 songs from the 2003 compilation by this acclaimed vocal quartet: Adonai • Can't Live a Day • Don't Save It All for Christmas Day • Everything to Me • Give It Up • Knockin' on Heaven's Door • New Day • Pray • Testify to Love • and more.
00306526 ....$16.95

JEREMY CAMP – RESTORED
All 12 tracks from the 2004 release: Be the One • Breathe • Even When • Everytime • Innocence • Lay Down My Pride • Letting Go • My Desire • Nothing Else I Need • Restored • Take You Back • This Man.
00306701................$16.95

CASTING CROWNS – LIFESONG
11 contemporary rock/worship songs from this popular band's 2005 album. Includes: And Now My Lifesong Sings • Does Anybody Hear Her • Father, Spirit, Jesus • In Me • Lifesong • Love Them like Jesus • Praise You in This Storm • Prodigal • Set Me Free • Stained Glass Masquerade • While You Were Sleeping.
00306748 ....$16.95

STEVEN CURTIS CHAPMAN – ALL THINGS NEW
Matching folio to the latest release from this perennial CCM favorite and multi-Dove Award winner. 12 songs, including: All Things New • Angels Wish • Believe Me Now • The Big Story • Coming Attractions • I Believe in You • Last Day on Earth • Much of You • Only Getting Started • Please Only You • Treasure of Jesus • What Now.
00306662 ....$14.95

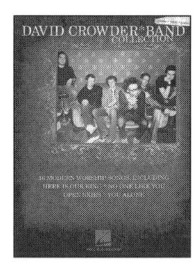

THE DAVID CROWDER*BAND COLLECTION
Based in Waco, Texas, David Crowder's innovative alt-pop style has made him one of today's most popular worship leaders. This collection includes 16 of his best songs: Here Is Our King • No One like You • Open Skies • Our Love Is Loud • You Alone • and more.
00306776 ....$16.95

FOR MORE INFORMATION, SEE YOUR LOCAL MUSIC DEALER, OR WRITE TO:

HAL•LEONARD® CORPORATION
7777 W. BLUEMOUND RD. P.O. BOX 13819 MILWAUKEE, WI 53213

For a complete listing of the products we have available, Visit us online at www.halleonard.com

DC TALK – INTERMISSION: THE GREATEST HITS
17 of DC Talk's best: Between You and Me • Chance • Colored People • Consume Me • Hardway (Remix) • I Wish We'd All Been Ready • In the Light • Jesus Freak • Jesus Is Just Alright • Luv Is a Verb • Mind's Eye • My Will • Say the Words • Socially Acceptable • SugarCoat It • Supernatural • What If I Stumble.
00306414 ....$14.95

BETHANY DILLON – IMAGINATION
16-year-old singer/songwriter/guitarist Bethany Dillon shows depth and talent beyond her years in this 2005 sophomore release. Includes 11 songs: Airplane • All That I Can Do • Be Near Me • Dreamer • Hallelujah • I Believe in You • Imagination • My Love Hasn't Grown Cold • New • Vagabond • The Way I See You.
00306745 ....$16.95

JENNIFER KNAPP – THE COLLECTION
15 songs from Knapp's greatest hits collection: Breathe on Me • By and By • Diamond in the Rough • Hold Me Now • Into You • Lay It Down • A Little More • Martyrs & Thieves • Refine Me • Romans • Say Won't You Say • Undo Me • The Way I Am • When Nothing Satisfies • Whole Again.
00306623 ....$14.95

KUTLESS – STRONG TOWER
The 2005 release by this Christian hard rock band hailing from Oregon includes 13 tracks: We Fall Down • Take Me In • Ready for You • Draw Me Close • Better Is One Day • I Lift My Eyes Up • Word of God Speak • Arms of Love • and more.
00306726................$16.95

Music Inspired by
THE CHRONICLES OF NARNIA
THE LION, THE WITCH AND THE WARDROBE
11 songs from the album featuring CCM artists performing songs inspired by the book and movie. Includes: I Will Believe (Nichole Nordeman) • Lion (Rebecca St. James) • Remembering You (Steven Curtis Chapman) • Waiting for the World to Fall (Jars of Clay) • and more.
00313311 ....$16.95

NEWSBOYS – DEVOTION
All 10 tracks from the 2004 recording by these alt CCM rockers: Blessed Be Your Name • Devotion • God of Nations • I Love Your Ways • Landslide of Love • Name Above All Names • The Orphan • Presence • Strong Tower • When the Tears Fall.
00306702................$16.95

NICHOLE NORDEMAN – BRAVE
11 tracks from the 2005 album by this talented singer-songwriter: Brave • Crimson • Gotta Serve Somebody • Hold On • Lay It Down • Live • No More Chains • Real to Me • Someday • We Build • What If.
00306729 ....$16.95

TWILA PARIS – HOUSE OF WORSHIP
Includes 12 songs: Christ in Us • Come Emmanuel • Fill My Heart • For Eternity • Glory and Honor • God of All • I Want the World to Know • Make Us One • Not My Own • We Bow Down • We Will Glorify • You Are God.
00306517 ....$14.95

PHILLIPS, CRAIG AND DEAN – LET YOUR GLORY FALL
10 songs from the 2003 release: Every Day • Fall Down • Hallelujah • Here I Am to Worship • How Deep the Father's Love for Us • Let Your Glory Fall • My Praise • Only You • What Kind of Love Is This • The Wonderful Cross.
00306519 ....$14.95

REBECCA ST. JAMES – IF I HAD ONE CHANCE TO TELL YOU SOMETHING
All 12 songs from this Aussie artist's 2005 album: Alive • Beautiful Stranger • Forgive Me • God Help Me • I Can Trust You • I Need You • Lest I Forget • Love Being Loved By You • Shadowlands • Take All of Me • Thank You • You Are Loved.
00306770 ....$16.95

SWITCHFOOT – NOTHING IS SOUND
Switchfoot's rock style and street-smart faith has given them widespread success in CCM and secular arenas. This songbook from their 2005 release features 12 songs: Daisy • Happy Is a Yuppie Word • Lonely Nation • The Setting Sun • Stars • more.
00306756 ....$16.95

THIRD DAY – WHEREVER YOU ARE
This popular rock band's 2005 release features "Cry Out to Jesus" plus: Carry My Cross • Communion • Eagles • How Do You Know • I Can Feel It • Keep on Shinin' • Love Heals Your Heart • Mountain of God • Rise Up • The Sun Is Shining • Tunnel.
00306766 ....$16.95

Prices, contents and availability subject to change without notice.

1205